MW01296653

Introduction

Export Compliance for Beginners

Who is this for? The person who is just starting out and knows absolutely *nothing* about shipping rules and government regulations. This is for the person who doesn't want to be thrown to the wolves but wants, or needs, to at least become familiar with some of the basics.

This book is not meant to go into full and complete complex details because there are so many rules with exemptions to rules and exceptions to exceptions, but to summarize where you can find the tools to do the job effectively with a few examples.

Consider this, when just starting out, it may feel as though the regulations have been written in such a way as to set someone up to fail. It will look as though it is convoluted to ensnare the new person and make them go nuts with worry. With pages of regulations tied to fines and jail time in both the EAR and the ITAR, there will be a small voice, somewhere inside, whispering, *It's a conspiracy to sell more headache and antacid medicines.*

Exporting can be perplexing and the terminology alone is not in layman terms. So what will this book cover that can help you? The importance of details, why EAR and ITAR are separate, using terminology and definitions. We'll go over the use of: CCL, ECCN, Categories, Denied Persons List, Prohibitions, the Country Chart. I'll summarize Carnets, Harmonized Tariffs and Schedule B. You'll be able to have a basic layout of where to start and things to look for when exporting. By the end, you will have a better grasp of how exporting works and where to begin looking for answers.

Chapter 1

Details, details, details

"Why do I need to know any of this stuff?" Good question. Here's your answer: to keep you out of jail and to not have hefty fines levied against you for doing something illegal, whether you mean to or not. Mistakes happen. Misinterpretation of regulations is one of the biggest issues facing logistics. Just because you reason out what you believe the interpretation of the regulation should mean, does not mean it will jibe with what the government may have in mind. It is always the best policy to document, document, document. No matter what you are shipping, whether it is a piece of paper or a bicycle or a mass spectrometer, keep track of it, in detail, in a folder. Document every decision and leave nothing out. If someone from the government comes to audit you, have everything handy, legible, and complete documentation of how you came to all of your decisions. They may take these items into account when asking why you chose to ship something under the EAR when they feel it should have been ITAR controlled or vice-versa. I'll say it again: document, document, document.

If you have a department that deals with your company's shipping and receiving then you do not need to know any of this, unless you want to better understand what they do, or you're part of the sales team and are trying to learn how to give better expectations to your clients. Remember, just because you haven't been caught yet or called out for it, doesn't make it legal; it means you've been very lucky.

I worked for years in a shipping department that almost never shipped the same thing twice in a year. Every item was unique and ranged from, "Okay, that's a nut and screw," to, "There's no specs on this. What in heaven's name is it?" Some items were the scientist's own creation which made it difficult, if not interesting, to figure out some of the shipping documentation. We always had to go back to the scientist to ask for specifications and get it in writing. If you don't have a place to start, start with, "What is it?"

Once you know about the item in question, there is a system in place to help guide you in your decision making on whether an item is in EAR or ITAR and in case it needs a license, if it has an exception or exemption available.

Chapter 2

Just isn't just

First, do yourself a favor right from the start, click your heels three times and say, "There's no such thing as *'just'*, There's no such thing as *'just'*. There's no such thing as *'just'*." Because there isn't. If you are shipping or receiving anything, that little word can get you into a big world of trouble. It's a word which is over used all the time. It degrades the value of the context and as a result, people end up trying to explain to the not so nice people with badges and handcuffs that it was all just a simple mistake of interpretation. "But it's just night-vision technology going to China. It's harmless." So says the person who sold the equipment to an embargoed country and wants to ship with no license. Don't worry, it's *just* lots of money tied up in fines, and *just* a few years jail time. I'm sure Bubba won't mind *just* sharing the jail cell. You should be *just* fine.

Save yourself the grief.

Get out of the habit of saying things like:

"We're just a University (or small business). It doesn't apply."

"We've been doing it this way for years. We'll just use the template."

"Just stuff the extra components around the items. We'll use them as filler."

"It's just a t-shirt. What's the big deal? It says made in the USA."

"Come on, it's just a satellite. We're not using it to spy on people. It's just for collecting weather data."

"It's just a 3D printer. How much harm can it possibly do?"

"It's just a radar for weather."

"Oh come on, we've worked with this guy for years. He's

just a scientist." Remember, it was *just* a scientist who created the atomic bomb.

"It's just an email. It's not like I'm shipping anything. "You're holding up the shipment. It's not like we're shipping a weapon. It's just a laser."

The <u>intent</u> of your item and its <u>end use</u> may be innocent or for research, but what the government looks at isn't just *just*. They look at *what* and *where* and *who*. Never say to yourself, "I'm just a scientist working at a university. This shipment is benign. Just ship it as is." Don't undersell yourself with the word *just*. Neither the State Department, the Department of Commerce, Defense Trade, nor Customs and Borders will not see it as *just*. Think of it like this, their job is to look at you and your shipment as though you're guilty first then work their way backward to decide whether or not you actually are a terrorist or an innocent person. They don't care about your status or who you work for, or your life's work and accomplishments. They are here to protect the nation's interests and all that it entails. Period.

Chapter 3

The devil is in the details

You've heard the adage, "The devil's in the details", and according to some, "It's better the devil you know than the one you don't." With exporting, it is true. The devil may lay in the minutia but it can land you with fines if not heeded. Keep good notes and better records. If audited, the government will ask you for shipment records within the last five years. Have a good export compliance program in place. If your company does not have one, consider requesting one be initiated to your boss. On one hand, If the manager still says no, there isn't much that can be done for them. You, on the other hand, need to comply with the government regulations so as not to have fines pop up or lose your export license from not keeping records or shredding them prior to the five-year mark.

Some shipments will be out of the country for more than five years. Even if the export file is closed officially, you need to keep the documents regarding the shipment in question available to any government agency requesting documentation until the export has concluded. Which means, if it has voluntary self-disclosure or other unique paperwork, you'll have to ask permission to shred these documents after the five year mark. Five years is the minimum to keep files on transactions. Some agencies may require you to keep them longer, depending on who has control over your commodity.

Here is a brief list of agencies most used and their policy on record retention:

Export Administration Regulations (EAR) 15 CFR 762

Electronic Export Information (EEI) 15 CFR 30.10, 15 CFR 30.15

International Traffic in Arms Regulations (ITAR) 22 CFR

122.5

Customs and Border Protection (CBP) 19 CFR 163.4

Office of Foreign Assets Control (OFAC) 31 CFR Part
501.601

Chapter 4

Everything means something

If you take nothing more from this book, I want the words 'document everything' to stick with you. It may sound dull and repetitive, but it can be of great service to you when, and if, you need it.

When reading a line, passage, paragraph or page from the EAR or ITAR, pay attention to every nuance. Take special care to notice anything in italics, Nota bene, bracketed, off set, astrict, bold print, or in quotation marks. Pay close attention to acronyms like NES (Not Elsewhere Specified) or NLR (No License Required) SME (Significant Military Equipment) as they represent more information which is available and it might affect your shipment. There are too many acronyms to go through but don't glance over them. Read and understand what they are and how they apply to what and where you are shipping.

Example:

EAR99 is a classification seen with the acronym NLR following as it is in a category in the Export Administration Regulations which says this particular item(s) is not listed with a specific ECCN (Export Control Classification Number) on the CCL (Commerce Control List). No license would be required if it meets all the criteria (General Prohibitions, etc).

Chapter 5

Stuff the stuff

Let's look at those examples from Chapter 1 for a moment.

"We're just a University (or small business). It doesn't apply." Universities and small businesses are like any other company or conglomerate and are held to the same rules and regulations as everyone else. They are not special and do not get special treatment. Even if they are a non-profit organization, they are still a company. Universities and other companies get dinged every year for export compliance regulation infractions because they told themselves they are just a university, they are just a scientist, they are just non-profit organization and it won't matter, or it's just scientific equipment. That word has caused so many problems for so many people. Even the small business owner needs to drop it from their vocabulary. They may believe they are exempt from the laws that govern shipping and receiving because of their size or lack of status. This is very far from the truth. Violations can range from the thousands to millions of dollars per incident and multiply for related infractions, no matter the size of your company or type.

Example:

Cite: University Charged with Export Control Violations - By: Thomas B. McVey & Jahna M. Hartwig; 05. 03. 2013
http://www.williamsmullen.com/news/university-charged-export-violations

"This case reinforces the important point that even universities engaged in fundamental research are required to comply with export control laws." In this instance, the university was shipping atmospheric testing equipment which was classified as EAR99 (ECCN EAR99 is the lowest possible export compliance control number that can be classified and labeled), but the place it was sent to was on the Denied Persons List. Just because your instruments, technology, paperwork, equipment, and/or research may be found as innocuous, there is still the questions of, "Where is it going?" and "Who is the recipient?" and "What will it be used for once it gets there?" Consequently, they learned an important lesson the hard way about keeping good records and not taking short cuts.

Example:

"Just stuff the extra components around the items. We'll use them as filler." Now the scientist and/or shipping department has decided to use up as much space as they can in their shipping crates to cut corners and save on the cost of the shipment. Let's say they want to fill part of the crates with nuts and bolts you can find at any store. Pretty generic. They may find them listed as EAR99 and decide it's no problem. But they weren't listed on the manifest, the Shipper's Export Declaration, and it wasn't listed on the license, and it wasn't included in the weight estimation of the shipment, and it was not listed on the invoice. Does it matter? Even the smallest thing can cause the biggest trouble. The item may not be worth much at first glance but Customs will look at the paperwork and decide your fate if everything, and I mean everything, isn't accounted for. It can lead to delays in shipping, having your shipment confiscated, more money thrown at the project for the delays, and much more. Export fines for incorrect paperwork can start at $10,000 per incident, but can vary depending on the destined country. Does that mean the nuts and bolts need to be on the invoice or accounted for after the fact? Not usually. But it is good practice to get into the habit of making sure all the I's are dotted and the T's are crossed.

Customs and Border Protection may perform spot checks on anything. It doesn't have to be something that automatically red flags the shipment as dangerous. Laptops have been confiscated and taken apart and held at Customs because it was part of the spot check, not because something was suspected or wrong. It is a way to keep things from entering or leaving the country under the radar.

Don't run the risk. Ship it separate or do what is necessary to correct the paperwork. If it's something that may, or will change the license, then don't be lazy. Contact the correct government department and ask them for guidance or help if you are uncertain of what paperwork is needed to amend the license.

*NOTE: Online, you can go to: www.Bis.doc.gov
Click on the middle section labeled: Would you like to: Speak to an Export Counselor
You'll find the phone numbers, email and address to write for more information.

The Bureau of Industry and Security puts out a book online every year titled "Don't Let This Happen to You". It's fascinating reading about all of the export control violations that occur all the time, from the really big ones you would swear you hear yourself saying, "Honestly, they didn't know better?" to the very minuscule where you hear yourself saying, "Really? I didn't know that!"

Example:

Item (what): night-vision technology (restricted by ITAR)
To (who): Bob the Terrorist (nice guy with shady connections)
At (where): Terrorist University, North Korea (company on Denied List; embargoed country)
End use (what): to mount on sniper rifles

I'm certain the United States government would frown upon sending out our night-vision technology controlled by ITAR, to a foreign person on the Denied Persons List, at a company known for terrorist activity, in a country on the Embargoed list, for the reason of putting said technology on a weapon to make it more useful to a person on the Denied Persons List.

Chapter 6

Well, that depends...

The next thing you will train yourself to say is, "It depends." as an answer for nearly everything. But be warned, for every time you say 'it depends' you need to have a solid avenue and documented answer to back it up, not guess work.

Here are things you may find yourself asking when working with a shipment:

Is this commodity something I can ship to Cuba, North Korea, Syria, Sudan, or Iran? The initial answer is no. Emphatically without question, no. There are 5 countries the United States is forbidden or restricted from doing business with. They are considered the T5 Countries or by the EAR definition, Country Code E (EAR Supplement 1 to Part 740 pages 1-7). Therefore, absolutely not. Or so you think. Well, that depends. "On what?" you might ask. It depends on whether you can apply for, and get, a license to legally send your item to that country. It depends on whether it is a humanitarian shipment. It depends on whether all the criteria can be met. And it depends on whether there is something going on in the world that hasn't been publicly announced (a coup, for instance).

Some things you will find yourself seeing the words no, definitely not, no way or even not in this life time, attached to it; and then you will hear the infamous words, "well, it depends." Be careful not to use those words manipulatively. Somewhat of the time, no means no. Period. But other times when the occasion is right, the government may look at the situation and say, "It's for a good humanitarian cause." and allow the shipment through with an exception. There are other reasons the government will allow a shipment through but be warned, you must meet all the criteria they set or it will most definitely be denied. If you ship it anyway, jail time and hefty fines await.

Chapter 7

There is no logic to any of this!

None of this makes sense. They say don't ship it at all to any of these embargoed places then they say under the right conditions you might be able. The rules say one thing but the interpretation may mean another. Even if you receive a judgment on an ECCN or Category and Title, when audited, the auditor may take a different stand on the interpretation and move forward with their investigation.

Take heart. Read thoroughly. Take notes. Document everything.

Start at the beginning and ask yourself the following same questions for all shipments: What is the object I am currently shipping? What will the end use be?
Who is it ultimately going to? Where is the end destination?

Why do these questions matter? Because each of these questions help determine the classification of the product and whether or not the item(s) *can* be shipped to the person and place, depending on the criteria.

Example: A shipper in the United Stated cannot ship nuclear weapons to anyone, or any company, or university in North Korea. Not even if someone were to say, "But, Bob's an old friend and he works for a university there. They just want to study its effects." Uhm. No. No. And emphatically, no. The United States government would look upon this poorly, to say the least. The probability of something like this shipping legally is next to zero, even if you went through very specific channels and sent requests to all the right people, it's not likely to happen.

The U.S. Government isn't trying to sabotage your ability

to work with other nations or limit your company's growth potential. It's looking out for the interest of the American people and all businesses and business practices there within. Their job is to protect national security, foreign policies, and U.S. Economic interests. If someone is to ship to an embargoed country, it means jumping through a lot of hoops and going through tons of red tape, just for the possibility. If the paperwork is wrong, it will be denied. If the license or paperwork is incomplete or information has been omitted, it will be denied, and sometimes fines occur. If the shipment goes out, and the license does not reflect accurately the intent, consignee (who is receiving it on the other end), address and correct item listing, it will be denied and possibly confiscated.

Chapter 8

What about Bob?

Foremost, the government doesn't care that you say you know Bob. If it turns out Bob's a terrorist, then they'll care a lot. What they care about is whether Bob is on the Denied Persons List. Which means, no matter how nice Bob is, that shipment isn't happening if he's on that list. And if you try to send it to one of his constituents as a work around, you're guilty of collusion. Which the government may take you to jail and fine you.

Next, even if Bob is a nice guy and not on the Denied Person List, you still have to contend with the fact your commodity is being shipped to a company or university outside the border of the United States of America. It is then considered "exported" when it leaves the country's boundaries. You may ask, "So what?" There is a LOT to the so what. There could be a book alone just on the so whats. The issue is, when it leaves the country borders, we no longer have full control over what happens to the shipment. We are putting our faith and trust in the hands of vendors and shippers, and carriers, and the people at Customs, and on the receiving end and the recipient. If the object in question is something benign like a letter of request or acknowledgment, it is under just as much scrutiny as nuclear proliferation material. Because it's leaving our borders, we must have as much documentation to prove our commodity's intent is legitimate and the paperwork is lawful.

Chapter 9

Who controls what?

These are the big three you will work with more often than not: EAR, ITAR, and OFAC.

EAR - Export Administration Regulations: regulates the exports of <u>commercial items</u> with potential military applications (dual-use). They are overseen by the U.S. Department of Commerce, Bureau of Industry and Security. Employ the use of <u>www.Bis.doc.gov</u> website to find the export control classification number on your commercial item to ship.

ITAR - International Traffic in Arms Regulations: regulates the exports of items and services <u>specifically designed for military applications</u>. They are overseen by the State Department and are responsible for international relations between the United States and other countries. The USML (United States Munitions List) is used to categorize your defense articles and some space-related technology.

OFAC - Office of Foreign Assets Control: per their site: <u>http://www.businessdictionary.com/definition/Office-of-Foreign-Asset-Control-OFAC.html</u> "A division of the United States Treasury department whose purpose is to enforce both trade and economic sanctions against groups and/or countries that are involved with terrorism and other types of dangerous or disreputable activities."

Agencies are very territorial when it comes to who controls what. When they occasionally have to work together, it means a lot of paperwork on all sides to represent why and who and what the process will involve. You can be certain where there is government policies involved, there will always be forms to fill out.

As for who controls what, if you have a commodity that

reasonably looks from the start to fall under Export Administration Regulations, it might. But, you may read and read until you find out it is actually controlled by the International Traffic in Arms Regulations division. It doesn't mean scrap the work you've done up until this point. It means keep all records of all activity including the work you did to arrive at this conclusion. In the end if you are audited and they ask for the paperwork on this shipment you'll be able to show them how you came to this decision. Especially if the definitions and terms are closely related and the regulations were not showing you definitively which one you should be in. Remember, ITAR will always trump EAR, but if your item truly belongs in EAR, don't immediately cast it aside and think, "Just go with ITAR all the time. It's safer." There's that word again, just; just getting us into trouble. I will repeat myself here, agencies are very territorial. If the item in fact belongs in EAR, by all means, treat it as such. Don't simply default to ITAR for everything. Everything does not belong there.

Where does OFAC come into play? OFAC's job is to plan and execute economic and trade sanctions. Trade sanctions are penalties applied by one country against another, restricting import/export activities. For instance, the trade sanctions the U.S. had imposed against Cuba for years was lifted on specific goods, not all, just some. Or more recently, the sanctions the EU is prepared to levy against Russia's state banks. So when you ship a commodity to another country, OFAC has a list of their own for blocked persons of interest and Specially Designated Nationals they check to be sure nothing illegal is transpiring. Activities may be subject to the US Government's economic sanctions against certain countries, entities and individuals. These sanctions programs are administered by the Treasury Department's Office of Foreign Asset Controls (OFAC).

How do I know if it's EAR https://www.bis.doc.gov/index.php/regulations/export-administration-regulations-EAR   or ITAR controlled https://www.pmddtc.state.gov/regulations_laws/ITAR.html ?

The Export Administration Regulations covers primarily commodities that are commerce related. Meaning, most of the items listed are going to be non-defense articles or non-military application. There are a few things, such as satellites, that have crossed-over or are shared between ITAR and EAR. So ready very carefully what your item description versus the definitions is in both. The rule of thumb is, if it was created with military applications in mind from the beginning, it is and will always remain, ITAR. The dead giveaway is in the name: International Traffic in *Arms* Regulations. Also, the word ITAR is in the word mil<u>itar</u>y.

An example:

You ask yourself, "But, I can purchase these nuts and bolts and screws at any hardware store. Why would they be considered ITAR controlled?" Here's an interesting one. It may be considered dual-use since it began its origin as a common nut, bolt, or screw. Its destiny changed when someone decided to change its physical specifications to fit that of a military device (like re-threading it). This makes it no longer something you can just purchase off the shelf. It has changed. It is now military specifications only. And, as we know, ITAR trumps EAR when it comes to these things. So, if you are having difficulty with things like dual-use items, make sure you contact the correct government agency and they will give you a judgment call on it. But make sure you get it in writing. Telling an official you got the judgment from Brenda in some division won't cut it when it comes to an audit.

Dot your I's. Cross your T's. Document everything.

Chapter 10

Definitions

When reading anything the government prints, you are always on the lookout for special meanings and implications. For instance, when reading about foreign persons in the export administration regulations, you may come across it in italics. This indicates the word has a special meaning and can be found in the definitions section of the EAR.

While definitions can be found at EAR 15 CFR Part 772.1 and ITAR 22 CFR Part 120, they can have a definite impact on your commodity shipment. For instance, you may ask, "What is a Foreign National?" EAR uses, but does not define, the term foreign national in its pages. Whereas both EAR and ITAR use the term *foreign person*. It is understood, extrapolating from both EAR Part 772 and ITAR 120.15, that the term foreign person covers any person who is not a U.S. Citizen, nor a permanent resident who holds a visa, nor protected by a granted status such as asylum. This also includes businesses and corporations who are not incorporated under U.S. Laws.

How would this apply to a shipment? The devil is in the details. Definitions can change over time and differ between the EAR and ITAR. Updates to them are done as soon as the information is available and notifications are sent out in their regards to the appropriate government agencies. Those sites are normally updated every twenty-four hours. During the time it takes to put together a shipment, the information can change. This affects a shipment most when it has already left the dock and is in transit. Meaning, if it's something that will change the wording and meaning of the documents attached to the shipment, then the shipment is wrong and needs to be called back to the loading dock where new and corrected paperwork must be available and ready to go. Has this ever happened? Yes. Does it happen often? No. Then why worry about it if it almost never happens? Because it does. Remember, the devil may be in the details but it's better the devil you know. If you allow the shipment to continue on its voyage *knowing* it's incorrect, and Customs and Borders Protection checks the paperwork versus the updates they received, and they see yours is wrong, they just may hold your shipment and contact you to let you know the shipment is being detained. If they find out you *knew* the shipment was wrong, they can fine you heavily.

Chapter 11

Consignee's role

In shipping, the consignee (buyer) is generally recognized as the person financially responsible for the shipment, sometimes known as the receiver. The consignor (seller) is usually the one shipping to the consignee.

The role of the consignee is to engage in financial and contractual agreements with a company from which they wish to purchase their commodity. In the case of universities, a consignee may not be purchasing anything from them. They may be borrowing scientific equipment or collaborating on a scientist's research. Even though they are not buying anything, they are still receiving something.

The consignee, if purchasing your commodity is from abroad, is considered a FPPI (Foreign Principal Party in Interest). The consignor is labeled the USPPI (United States Principal Party in Interest).

Contracts are drawn up to convey the interests between the FPPI and the USPPI.. Specifically the contract should note the financial obligations of the consignee and shipping details. Who is the consignee? Where is it ultimately being routed to? What is the commodity and how much of the items is being shipped?

According to the Foreign Trade Regulations (FTR) found in 15 CFR Part 30, in a routed transaction the FPPI is required to provide a power of attorney or written statement (which can also be in an email) authorizing either the USPPI or authorized U.S. Agent to prepare and file the Electronic Export Information (EEI) using the Automated Export System (AES).

The consignee will take possession of the commodity when it has cleared Customs and arrives at the final destination.

Now in English: A person (buyer/consignee) in another country (foreign person) is purchasing something (commodity) from a person in the United States (consignor). A contract is drawn up describing what is going to take place. The foreign person (FPPI) will have the American (USPPI) ship the item (commodity) to a warehouse they own in another country (destination). The American will put together the EEI. The freight forwarder can and usually will, submit the EEI on behalf of the USPPI using the AES online. The commodity ships. The receiver (consignee) signs for it. An email is sent saying thank you for your business. And all of this is filed away for five years. On to the next shipment.

Chapter 12

Embargoes and Denied Persons List

What exactly is an embargo and how does a country get put on the 'does not play well with others' list?

An embargo is any official ban or regulation placed on trade with another country. For any number of reasons, an embargo may be put in place. If the country does not agree with another country's religious or economic standings, or government policies on terrorism.

How do you know if the country you're dealing with is embargoed? www.bis.doc.gov and the EAR Part 746 as well. There are many places that can be found online with lists. The official listing for ITAR is found at eCFR's website: https://www.pmddtc.state.gov/embargoed_countries/index.html

Why use two separate sites for EAR and ITAR embargoed countries? Even though both the EAR and ITAR cover most of the same countries and entities, ITAR has a list of "proscribed countries" that carry the list a step further. Proscribed countries in this instance is considered embargoed nations or those with sanctions against them, only the list is longer for ITAR controlled commodities. This list is significantly more expansive than just the Prohibitions or Denied Persons List, due to the nature of exporting defense articles.

Is there any software or websites available that can be used to get most or all of the information for your international checklist of entity, place, and country? www.bis.doc.gov is free and updated generally every twenty-four hours. There are websites and software packages available. For instance, places like Visual Compliance offer ECCN and USML classifications, OFAC screening, Denied Persons List and more. There is a yearly subscription rate for this site. However, something like this is a good tool to use, if you can find one within your company's budget.

Chapter 13

Is it Foreign National or Foreign Person?

What is the difference between using the term 'foreign national' and 'foreign person'? These terms are interchangeable when addressing a situation when a person is from another country. The difference is when using the terms found in the EAR and ITAR definitions.

Earlier in Chapter 10 we noticed the definitions found at EAR 15 CFR Part 772.1 and ITAR 22 CFR Part 120, are similar in that the EAR uses, but does not define, the term foreign national. Instead, it as well as ITAR, refers to anyone who is not a U.S. Citizen as a *foreign person*.

When technical data or technology is transferred to a foreign person, it is considered a "deemed" export. However, if either of those is categorized as public domain then "deemed" does not apply, because anyone can get the information anywhere. "Deemed" export simply means you need an export license before you can release *controlled* technology to a foreign person. This information can be found at www.bis.doc.gov .

When it comes to releasing controlled technology or data, the law if very specific. The Commerce Control List (CCL) 15 CFR 730 -774 Supplement 1 and ITAR USML 22 CFR 121 give the parameters of what is considered technology and how to approach it best.

Chapter 14

Do I need a license?

Ask yourself, "What am I shipping?" and "Where is the commodity going?" If you answer, "I don't know." then you're being honest. Never guess at what you think you might be shipping.

This may sound repetitive but, if your item is categorized as a defense article, then yes most definitely it will require a license to ship. If it is of commercial, dual-use, or deemed an export, then yes you will require a license.

There are different types of licenses available. Too many to go through here but suffice to say, when you are ready to put the information into either SNAP-R (EAR) or DTrade (ITAR), they have the types listed. Read often. Read thorough. Ask questions.

All three, EAR and ITAR and OFAC carry both civil and criminal penalties for export violations. While each may differ in what the violation is and the penalty incurred for it, they all carry steep fines and often jail time.

If you need a license for anything, don't huff, roll your eyes, sag your shoulders or feel the need to scream or cry. Once you know you need one, look for the exception or exemption. Remember, a license is a good thing; it is documentation that the commodity is being shipped legally. An exception or exemption is there to assist or ease the process. Do not cut corners. Document everything. I think you already guessed that.

Chapter 15

Prohibitions

Why and when do we use Prohibitions? Prohibitions are used in the EAR when we know the ECCN (Export Control Classification Number) and country to which it is being shipped.

At this point, if the CCL (Commerce Control List) hasn't thrown us over to ITAR, then the ECCN shows it belongs to EAR. The CCL will have Reasons for Control such as MT (Missile Technology), or AT (Anti-Terrorism) showing they want you to look up two things: 1) continue reading in the CCL to be sure there is no exception listed already; 2) look at the Country Chart and find the country it is being sent to. https://www.bis.doc.gov/index.php/forms-documents/doc_view/14-commerce-country-chart. Then look across the page to the columns labeled MT and AT. If there is an X in either box, the shipment requires a license. No need to go to the General Prohibitions at this point. But, if the CCL shows the ECCN has nothing prohibiting it, and the Country Chart has nothing restricting it in any of the columns, then we are *required* to look at all ten Prohibitions.

EAR 15 CFR Part 736.2 is the in-depth information for what to expect of the Prohibitions list. If your commodity or item meets any of the criteria, it needs a license. If you've come this far and it hasn't needed one yet, and none of the Prohibitions apply, then you don't require a license, but you are still required to document your exception and/or findings.

Sound convoluted? The EAR is recognized as something a little more complex in how it treats its requirements than say ITAR. ITAR is renowned for being relatively straight forward.

Chapter 16

Dual-Use

We already know the Department of Commerce oversees the EAR. We also know anything military or considered a defense article and falls under ITAR. But what about those oddities that is both a commercial or civilian commodity that can also qualify for military use? These items are called dual-use. Per the EAR CFR 15 Part 774, a list of these items can be found on the Wassenaar Arrangement Munitions List http://www.wassenaar.org/control-lists/. The Wassenaar Arrangement Munitions List, however, doesn't cover software or technology.

There are very few dual-use items which will require a license from the Bureau of Industry and Security (BIS). Most of the items which will fall under the instructions of the EAR will be what is called 'tangible' items like software, and technology.

Tangible items, according to 15 CFR 772 means: "...fixed in any tangible medium of expression." Examples of this are: drawings, photos, blueprints, prototypes, 3D models, manuals, or disks. Things you can touch. As opposed to 'intangible' which is services or training. Things you cannot physically touch.

What we do know about dual-use is that it rarely ever comes up but when it does it most likely falls under the EAR, except where the item began as a military product which makes it ITAR, or if it is on the WAML. Then again, it all depends.

Chapter 17

Why is it so convoluted?

Here is where I take a deep breath and try to get into a more zen mode. This question has been asked a million times and not once has anyone ever been able to answer it with any real rhyme or reason other than, "That's just how it was written." or my favorite, "They are just trying to make money from businesses any way they can. If they can trip us up, they make dough." Which sounded like a better reason than any of the others since the legal language could very well use an overhaul and become more simplified. Not everyone who reads the regulations is a lawyer but you always feel like part of you must be.

People who have been working with export compliance for a majority of their career will tell you, "It's all about experience. You just have to get experience." My pet peeve. That little word 'just'; it seems to pop up and ruin everything. Those with the experience tend to forget that those without it were not born with the benefit of the knowledge they've acquired over their life. Nor do they realize that little word 'just' can land a person with little to no knowledge in jail and/or steep in civil and criminal fines.

So, why is it so convoluted? Why can't all sides get together and make one dictionary of terms and agree on them? Why can't they use the Webster's Dictionary? It's already in circulation and has been for a long time. Why can't their terms be the same as a relatively normal dictionary? For example, the ITAR uses "exemption" and the EAR uses "exceptions". The concept is the same. You're looking for something to release you legally from getting a license based on certain criteria. http://dictionary.reference.com/browse/exception?s=t

The dictionary refers to exception as: "something excepted; an instance or case not conforming to the general rule." But it refers to exemption as: "...implies special privilege or freedom from imposed requirement."

The EAR defines exception as: "...determination that no license is required."

The ITAR defines exemption as: "A specific reason as cited within this part that eliminates the requirement for filing EEI." (15 CFR Part 30 Definitions).

The ITAR does not use the term exception but within the EAR pages you may come across the word exemption.

If the terms mean the same thing then why do we have to look in so many places to get the same answer?

I hope we were paying attention earlier when I said, "Agencies are very territorial when it comes to who controls what." It is no different when they write their rules and regulations.

As part of the Export Control Reform process, in the year 2015, there were a considerable number of proposals to integrate or revamp some of the terminology between the ITAR and the EAR where some of the verbage will be closer in definition.

Reform takes time. Arduous and sometimes clunky, but at least they are trying.

Chapter 18

Can't they just write in plain English?

What is an export? Anything that leaves the United States boarders. If you are already starting your sentence with, "What about..." then you have missed the point. Anything that leaves.the boarders. Anything: Email, physical items, papers, documents, software, hardware, if it leaves the boundaries of the United States, then it is an export.

According to the EAR 15 CFR Part 772: Export is defined as: "... an actual shipment or
transmission of items out of the United States." The ITAR has a much longer description: "Sending or taking a defense article out of the United States in any manner, except by mere travel outside of the United States..." It goes on for six more paragraphs detailing every nuance.

Then why didn't they simply write the obvious? The EAR put it as blunt and brief as they could and were still able to get the point across. The ITAR is more defined because when it comes to national security and shipping out something that might be construed as military or a defense article, they want everything possible covered. No one would be able to legally come back to them and say, "That was never in there." or "Look it up. If it's not written, it is opinion only." Such controversy has no place where national security is concerned. It does not mean the EAR is lackadaisical or less effective in its wording. It means the EAR does not export military or defense articles and thereby does not require such in-depth remarks. When they say, 'anything' leaving the borders, that is exactly what they mean with no room for argument. No "What if..." No "How about..." No "What about this?" That includes both tangible and intangible.

Chapter 19

CCL and Categories

This might be easier if you can actually see what I'm talking about so I've included BIS's website and where the information can be found regarding the CCL on the EAR:

https://www.bis.doc.gov/index.php/regulations/commerce-control-list-ccl
15 CFR Supplement 1 to Part 774

CCL, otherwise know as the Commerce Control List, is operated by the Department of Commerce. Remember them? The Export Administration Regulations division that deals primarily with commercial commodities and dual-use items. The CCL is used to classify a commodity or item by assigning it an ECCN (Export Control Classification Number). If your product is too low on the consumer goods list it is considered EAR99.

*NOTE: Never believe for one moment because an item or commodity is listed as EAR99 that it automatically does not need a license. You still have the General Prohibitions to deal with and the Denied Persons List. An item can be EAR99 and still need a license.

The CCL is a comprehensive list of 10 categories and 5 product groups. The Categories are numbered 0-9 and the Groups are A-E.

It looks something similar to this:

0 - Nuclear & Miscellaneous
1 - Materials, Chemicals, Micro organisms and Toxins
2 - Materials Processing
3 - Electronics
4 - Computers

5 Part 1 - Telecommunications

A - Systems, Equipment and Components
B - Test, Inspection and Production Equipment
C - Material

When classifying your commodity, you will need those specifications we spoke of earlier. The specifications may have the ECCN already listed which will cut down your time on needing to classify it. However, do not take it at face value that the ECCN they have listed is correct. Use it as a guideline. Check it out for yourself. Some companies make a template and it never gets updated. Since you are the responsible party shipping the commodity, you will need to dot your I's and cross your T's and of course, document everything.

Now, if your commodity is being looked up on the USML (United States Munitions List), you will find the wording and layout quite different.

http://www.ecfr.gov/cgi-bin/text-idx?node=pt22.1.121
USML Title 22 Part 121

The USML is divided into 21 Categories of articles represented by Roman Numerals. For example, Category I (1) is Firearms, Category XIII (13) is Auxiliary military Equipment and Category XXI (21) is Miscellaneous Articles. Within the USML the Categories have notations for special definitions. They use an asterisk to denote if an article is considered "significant military equipment" (SME). There is no ECCN or CCL. There is no General General Prohibitions. There are only regulations and exemptions.

Even though the USML is very straight forward, it can still be tough to classify your commodity. Something that may help to remember is if it was created for military purposes or created to enhance existing military defense articles, it is ITAR related through and through.

Chapter 20

ECCN versus Categories

"Why can't I use my ECCN on my defense article or my Category on my commercial item? I've already looked it up." As stated previously, "Agencies are very territorial when it comes to who controls what." The Federal Government is keen on making sure their I's are dotted and their T's are crossed so there is little room for confusion or arguments. Unfortunately, the terminology can be daunting and feel like circular logic; constantly saying something without saying anything.

While it would be nice to have a crossover between ITAR and EAR, there is almost no room. The EAR is designated for commercial use. The ITAR is especially designed for defense articles. Hence the division and keeping them separate for census bureau purposes. It makes it easier for Customs and Borders to keep track of the information leaving the country. A tally of the traffic of what comes and goes helps to identify how much harm or good the United States sanctions and laws are doing locally and worldwide.

Keeping them separate is a good idea, even if it is sometimes difficult to keep the terminology straight. But remember to dot your I's, cross your T's, ask questions and document everything.

Chapter 21

Exception versus Exemption

What happens if I use the term exception when I mean exemption when talking about ITAR? For some odd reason, certain people in the export industry get their hackles raised when you interchangeably use exception and exemption incorrectly in a sentence. They know what you're talking about but the terminology gets stuck in their craw and they have no compunction about correcting you on its use.

If you're new to exporting, it will do you well to try very hard to get the terminology straight, right off the bat. When talking to government officials, they want to help you but if they don't know if you're still talking about the EAR or ITAR when switching terms in mid-sentence, they will be confused. They understand you're new, but they too will correct you on term usage.

Ever order a Big Mac and you get a Quarter Pounder? They're the same, right? They're both equally hamburgers. But they are not the same. If you order a generic hamburger, you never know what you might get. You may be talking about the same thing but to get something specific, you have to tell them exactly what you're talking about. If you're not sure what the terminology is, let the person know up front so they are aware to listen for key elements when chatting with you. If you want help, be helpful.

Here's the difference in an exception and an exemption. An exception is used in the EAR when a license is required but the conditions can be met to qualify the commodity for an authorization to ship without the license. Be warned, all conditions _must_ be met.

An exemption is used in the ITAR in much the same way. It relaxes the conditions for a ITAR controlled defense article to leave the country (ITAR Part 126.3-126.5).

For instance:

We have trade relations with Canada. If we were to ship a defense article to Canada, it would need a license because it is classified as a military item. However, there is a Canadian exemption for certain items that will relax the conditions since they are the Unites States' ally.

We would like to keep things simpatico with our neighboring countries. To keep in good-standing, the United States have trade agreements that assist in shipping among friendly countries.

Chapter 22

Country Chart

Is there a flow to this? It doesn't seem so at first. The EAR is a bit more complex with all the tools you have to use just to see if your item *can* leave the country. But once you have your commodity classified, you'll go to the next step, finding out if the country you want to send it to is prohibited.

The Commerce Country Chart, found in Supplement 1 Part 738 of the EAR, is used after classifying your commodity or item. When you have gone through the CCL and found your ECCN, the number will have Reasons for Control listed in it. The Reason for Control tells us why we cannot ship to this country.

The list ranges from Chemical and Biological Weapons to Anti-terrorism. On the left of the chart is listed the names of the countries while across the top is the range of Reasons for Control. If there is an X provided in any of the squares where the ECCN has listed a Reason, then the shipment needs a license and you will need to look for an exception. If no X is provided, then *in this step*, no license is required. If no license is required at this step, go to your General Prohibitions and check through them next.

https://www.bis.doc.gov/index.php/forms-documents/doc_view/14-commerce-country-chart

See? There is a flow.

Chapter 23

SED, EEI, AES Filing

Now to confuse you.

What was an SED is now the EEI applied on the AES by the USPPI for a FPPI. My gods the government loves their acronyms.

SED stands for Shipper's Export Declaration - it was a manual way (hand-written waybill) to declare commodities being exported valued at $2500 or more. This declaration is now called EEI and done electronically through the AES system.

EEI stands for Electronic Export Information - The parameter is still the same: commodities over $2500 classified under Schedule B or when a license is required is required to be file electronically. If the company or person (USPPI) or foreign person (FPPI) cannot file electronically, the freight forwarder can do so but a power of attorney is required. The carrier will file the EEI on behalf of the USPPI through AES to Customs and Border Protection (CBP).

AES is the Automated Export System - the electronic system used to file the EEI. According the 15 CFR Title 15 Part 30, the Foreign Trade Regulations, this information is mandatory when exporting.

https://aesdirect.census.gov/

AES is used for both the EAR and ITAR for filing.

That wasn't so bad.

Chapter 24

Canada, like Mexico, is its own country

We've all heard Mufasa tell his son, "Everything the light touches is our kingdom." That doesn't include Mexico and Canada. The light stops there. Canada and Mexico *share* our borders but are *not* part of the United States. You'd be surprised how many people are under the impression because our borders touch, they believe they belong to the United States. Canada's known for being friendly but they aren't *that* friendly. The same goes for the rest of the planet. Simply because borders are shared with friendly and unfriendly nations does not mean we can ship anything, any time, any where just because we're allies or because we want to.

It is noteworthy to mention here that the United States has free trade agreements between both Canada and Mexico. Under NAFTA (North American Free Trade Agreement), the trilateral agreement among United States and Mexico and Canada has, in the past, was supposed to allow for economic growth opportunities and boosted competitiveness in the global markets. In recent studies, they are reevaluating whether that concept still holds true. The model NAFTA created was the framework for many other trade agreements between countries. While it is a solid foundation, it can still use some tweaking.

Chapter 25

Carnet

Finally! Something that makes sense. A passport for your goods to travel within a country and not have to reapply for a license all the time or pay duties and taxes coming and going. So, what is a Carnet and how does it work?

A Carnet is also known in the industry as a "temporary passport" for goods and commodities. The key word is *temporary*. Temporary means the item or goods is going out for less than a year and returning, or is a 'not for sale' item like a sample that would be staying in the country of destination.

How long is a Carnet good for? It depends. Where is it going? What is it for? These questions can help determine if it will only be gone for 6 months or up to 1 year. Asking, those two questions helps to determine the time frame it is allowed to be gone due to the nature of the individual country's policy on temporary imports.

When can I use a Carnet? Carnets are most commonly used for shipping trade show material and exhibitions, but also waives the duties and VAT (Value Added Taxes) of other commodities into another country.

*NOTE: A Carnet <u>does not</u> replace a license. You still need to classify your material.

For more information regarding Carnets, I suggest visiting the professionals at:

http://www.atacarnet.com/what-carnet

Chapter 26

Harmonized Tariffs and Schedule B

What is the difference in Harmonized Tariffs and Schedule B? Aren't they really the same thing? Actually, one is for import and the other is for export.

Allow me to explain...

Per http://export.gov/california/sanfrancisco/qa/hssb/, and I quote: "Harmonized System (HS) numbers are used to classify products for customs purposes. By international agreement, most countries recognize the same first 6 "harmonized" digits..." The Harmonized Tariff System (HS) is for imports only.

"Schedule B Numbers are used to classify exported products from the United States and are based on the international HS system. HS numbers and Schedule B numbers will be the same up to the first 6 digits as the importing country's classification code."

Couldn't have said it better myself.

*NOTE: HS Tariffs and Schedule B numbers are used by the Census Bureau to disseminate the most up-to-date information about duties and taxes for the shipper to use. They also use this information for official statistics reports on the exports of goods from the United States.

The information gathered and redistributed keeps the records up to date regularly. It also allows for the data gathered to show whether the United States has more of one type of commodity than another to specific places. This allows the government agencies to act accordingly to adjust their laws and trade agreements.

Chapter 27

Keeping records

If you're old enough to know what a vinyl record is, you're old enough to know that keeping something that ancient is useless. It may have sentimental value but as time goes by, it has been replaced by discs, mp3 players and now the 'cloud'. Keeping something of value based on sentimentality is one thing, keeping records valued at only a few years is another.

Keep your records clean. Be wary of keeping things past 7 years. The files can become quite bloated and take up a great deal of room. If your company has a policy of keeping them longer, oblige the rules. If not, then set up a record keeping system that is efficient and requires very little maintenance.

Point blank, record keeping is for 5 years from the date of export. Well, that depends. According to bot the EAR and the ITAR, all records must be kept for 5 years from the date of the license expiration. Well, almost all records. It can be confusing what you must and don't have to keep after the 5 year grace. However, any government agency has the right to request proof of your record shipping and export transactions, cradle to the grave, so to speak. It is prudent to double check what can and cannot be retained for audit purposes, up to and including the 5 year mark.

What happens if I don't keep all the records up to the 5 year mark? Steep fines and civil and potential criminal penalties occur. In the least, businesses have lost their export license for not keeping good records when audited.

Chapter 28

A complete rundown

Part 1

*NOTE: Due to the sheer length of this chapter, it has been broken down into parts.

Have everything you need available to lessen errors and hasten response times.

Remember: Due diligence; details, details, details and document, document, document.

Read carefully. Everything means something. Take special care if the information is in anything other than a regular font. Don't discount or ignore it if you don't recognize or understand it. Look it up and ask questions.

Take no chances. The consequences can be steep.

Have your bookmarks available for ITAR and EAR definitions. You will find the links listed on the last page of the book and scattered throughout where referenced.

By knowing these things before you begin, it will help with the flow:

1. <u>What</u> is it? Identify the item or product. Get all specifications and contracts regarding the item or product and transaction ahead of time. Clarify any miscommunication or likely issues.

2. <u>Where</u> is it going? Get a solid address, no partials. Country? Township? University? Company? Is the company held by a U.S. corporation?

3. <u>Who</u> is the ultimate recipient? Acquire their full name, no partials and no abbreviations. Do ***NOT*** under any circumstance try to find a work around for this. If Bob in Syria is who you're sending it to and they are on the Denied Persons List, don't believe for one moment the government is okay with sending it to one of his colleagues in lieu of this. It means you are attempting to circumvent the issue. If the person's name is not on the original contract or documentation okaying the transaction, then it is illegal to do so because you knew ahead of time, and knowingly tried to circumvent the law. It's considered defrauding the government and highly frowned upon.

4. <u>End use</u>. What is it ultimately being used for? What is its end purpose? If you have an item that was created from the beginning as a military item, it most likely will remain such. No matter if it has been refit for civilian use or scientific research. It was created for military, it stays military and most likely remains in ITAR. A rose by any other name is still a flower.

Part 2

5. <u>Denied Persons List</u>. If your company uses a program like Visual Compliance or Bis.doc.gov, you will need to look up the Denied Parties List and check to see if any of this information shows up flagged. If ANY of it does, the shipment ends before it begins.

Why? Let's look at Bob from Syria again. Let's pretend his name is Bob Smith and was born and works in Syria for a Nuclear Research facility. If his name is found on the Denied Parties List, he has been denied by the government. He's on the list for a reason. If he's fine but the company he works for, Nuclear Research facility, is listed, the shipment ends. Same reason. It's on the list. If he's okay, and the company is okay but the country or address is embargoes or on the list, it will not ship. The only way it has a chance at this point is if you can prove beyond a shadow of a doubt, this Bob Smith is not the person on the list, the company is not the same one, and the country cannot be on the embargoed list. If any of them are, none of it goes.

The country is the one you cannot get around. At this point, you need to speak with the sales person and review the contract to be certain all information is correct, especially spelling. The misspelling of a name, address, company or country can start this whole process and bring it to a halt.

If everything passes and is clear, document it. All of it. No matter how inane; have it on file how you came to the conclusion this person, place, and country is okay, then you can continue the shipment.

6. <u>Classify it.</u> Now we can find out if it is EAR or ITAR related. You probably have a good inclination by now if you have the specifications in hand. Most of the time, if it's an item from a manufacturer, they have the specs and classification available. If not, you will have to either call or contact the

manufacturer online, or ask the government nicely for a ruling using SNAP-R, http://www.bis.doc.gov/, or an export counselor at http://www.bis.doc.gov/index.php/about-bis/contact-bis, or try to classify it yourself (CCL or USML). This includes finding out if it is a dual-use item.

If it is EAR, you will need to find the ECCN (the reason for control) in the CCL (Commerce Control List) Supplement 1 to Part 774 https://www.bis.doc.gov/index.php/regulations/export-administration-regulations-EAR .
Commercial items are regulated by the Department of Commerce.

If it is ITAR, you will need to look up the USML and find the Category   http://www.ecfr.gov/cgi-bin/text-idx?node=pt22.1.121. The USML consists of military items, articles, services and technical data and therefore regulated by the Department of State.

Start with the assumption it's ITAR first, if you're not certain. If it's not and you look it up, somewhere in the pages it will toss you to EAR. The same for EAR, if you're not supposed to be in there, most of the time it will toss you back over to USML.

*NOTE: USML *always* trumps EAR.

Example for EAR:

Let's look up the ECCN in the CCL for a computer.

Under A. "End Items," "Equipment," "Accessories" etc. 4A001 it says under the license requirements that the Reason for Control is: NS, MT, AT, NP
The Control(s) specify you must look at the Country Chart https://www.bis.doc.gov/index.php/forms-documents/doc_view/14-commerce-country-chart to be sure none of these Reasons for Control have an X next to them in the

country listed. If there is an X, you MUST get a license or have an exception to that license.

Let's say it was Canada. Next to it under NS (National Security) there is no X. For MT (Missile Technology) there is no X. For AT (Anti-Terrorism) there is no X. For NP (Nuclear Proliferation) There is no X. Therefore you need no license, so no exception. Also assuming it has passed the General Prohibitions as well (15 CFR 736.2 https://www.bis.doc.gov/index.php/forms-documents/doc_view/413-part-736-general-prohibitions).

But what if it's a dual-use item? Something that has both commercial and military application is considered dual-use. Again, ITAR will always trump EAR, especially when it comes to dual-use items. A special license may be required. Start at the beginning if you are uncertain what to do ask about a dual-use item. What is the item and what is its purpose?

*NOTE: Read more on dual-use goods and technologies under the Wassenaaar Arrangement. http://www.wassenaar.org/

Part 3

7. <u>General Prohibitions</u>. If it is classified as EAR, you need to be sure it doesn't clash with any of the ten General Prohibitions. If it does, you will need a license and therefore look for an exception. (https://www.bis.doc.gov/index.php/forms-documents/doc_view/413-part-736-general-prohibitions)

8. <u>Exceptions or Exemptions.</u> Once you know what the classification is, the regulations will tell you whether this needs to be licensed or not. If it is, look to see if there is an exception or exemption available.

If it is subject to the EAR, look at 15 CFR 732 - Steps for Using the EAR, to determine if you need a license.

If the item falls under EAR, look to 15 CFR 736.2 - General Prohibitions to find out if it qualifies for an exception under these.

Part 740 allows you to export items subject to the EAR that would otherwise require a license under the General Prohibitions.

Be warned: read everything. Everything prior and everything after a section. For example, if you were to read 15 CFR 740 but not all the way through 740.2, you wouldn't realize that license exceptions in EAR may have limitations. Read thoroughly.

If your item falls under ITAR jurisdiction, go to the USML http://www.ecfr.gov/cgi-bin/text-idx?node=pt22.1.121

9. If a <u>license</u> is required for:

EAR - use SNAP-R https://snapr.bis.doc.gov/snapr/ You will need to register with them first if you or your company hasn't already https://snapr.bis.doc.gov/registration/Register.do

(Part 748 for support documentation and Part 750 for the license review process)

ITAR - use DTrade
https://www.pmddtc.state.gov/DTRADE/index.html in the right column at the top click DTrade2 Log-In. You will need to be registered with them
http://pmddtc.state.gov/DTRADE/documents/Getting_Started_Instructions.pdf .

Part 4

10. <u>Free Trade Agreements</u>. Do we have a trade agreement with the country it is destined, to assist with the tariffs and harmonized code?

Example: NAFTA (North American Free Trade Agreement) helps lift customs tariffs on goods traveling across the borders of the United States, Canada, and Mexico. A Certificate of Origin must be produced to qualify goods under the Agreement.

11. <u>Invoice</u>. Create from a template your company may already have or customize one for the different types of shipments.

12. <u>Harmonized Codes or Schedule B.</u>
http://www.export.gov/logistics/eg_main_018119.asp
Harmonized Tariff Schedule (HTS) - The US *import* classification system. https://www.usitc.gov/tata/hts/index.htm

Schedule B - is a 10 digit number used only in the United States to classify physical goods for *export* to another country. http://www.census.gov/foreign-trade/schedules/b/index.html

HTS - 6 digit it's all based on. To classify *Import*.

*NOTE: Needed for tariff rates and whether a product qualifies for preferential tariff under a Free Trade Agreement.

Part 5

12. <u>Power of Attorney</u>. A power of attorney or written authorization is used when a Foreign Principal Party of Interest (FPPI) acts on behalf of the US (USPPI) shipper and assumes all responsibilities associated, unless otherwise specified in the contract and written authorization forms.

13. <u>EEI</u> (Electronic Export Information). Formerly known as the Shipper's Export Declaration, is filed when the value of a commodity being shipped under Schedule B is over $2500. <u>https://help.cbp.gov/app/answers/detail/a_id/292/~/when-to-apply-for-an-electronic-export-information-%28eei%29</u>

For example:

If you are shipping through FedEx, their website or software will have an area available for you to click and choose whether you are creating your own invoice or if you want them to do it for you. The EEI will have a pull down menu to choose what the best description fits your item.

14. <u>AES (Automated Export System)</u>. As stated at: <u>http://www.cbp.gov/trade/trade-community/automated/aes/about</u> , "AES is a conduit through which required export shipment information reaches the appropriate agency." This electronic process is used when the exporter or USPPI, or authorized agent, is ready to ship. The exporter enters the (EEI) information using the AES where it is checked for accuracy and data reporting, such as: checking for previously approved military shipment licenses, then transmits the information to the Directorate of Defense Trade Controls where they validate the shipment against past shipments. The carrier usually files this with the US Customs and Border, but you, the shipper, are responsible for the EEI.

Part 6

15. <u>Shipping</u>: Is it a <u>Carnet</u>? Will the item(s) or product(s) be leaving the country temporarily and returning? A Carnet allows this to happen as long as the item(s) and/or product(s) are to be re-exported within 12 months. (19 CFR Part 114 www.gpo.gov)

*NOTE: a Carnet may be used if the item(s) and/or product(s) are not on the Denied Parties List nor going to an embargoed country.

*NOTE: if it's *consumable* or *not* returning, then it's not *temporarily* leaving the country.
http://export.gov/logistics/eg_main_018129.asp

*NOTE: the fees for getting a Carnet depend on the value of the shipment.
http://www.exhibitoronline.com/topics/article.asp?ID=147<u>3</u>

If the item in question is considered "significant military" or "unclassified military" under the USML, a DSP may be used.

22 CFR Part 123 also found on DTrade
https://www.pmddtc.state.gov/DTRADE/index.html

DSP-5: <u>Permanent</u> *export* of unclassified defense articles or unclassified technical data.
DSP-6: *Amendment* to DSP-5; used when adding a freight forwarder, there are errors in the paperwork, a change in commodities, or a change in location, or the license has changed.
DSP-61: <u>Temporary</u> *import* of unclassified defense articles or unclassified technical data.
DSP-62: *Amendment* to DSP-61; used when there is a change in the name/address, paperwork errors (spelling),

changes in part numbers, change in ultimate destination, or license.

DSP-73: <u>Temporary</u> *export* of unclassified defense articles or unclassified technical data.

DSP 74: *Amendment* to DSP-73. Used when adding or changing U.S. Freight forwarder, paperwork error (spelling), changes in license.

DSP-83: Export or temporary *import* of <u>classified</u> defense articles or classified technical data.

16. Record Keeping. Document, document, document - everything. Keep a good copy you can pull up at a moment's notice if you need to refer back to it or if you are being audited. Hold on to them for a minimum of 5 year for both EAR and ITAR.

Did you get all that? Okay. It's time to ship!

And this was only *some* of the basics.

Chapter 29

Tools to do the job

If you're the owner of a business and just starting in logistics, or are about to start classes in export compliance and it all seems overwhelming, check out the following links and shortcuts I've created. They are helpful when beginning in logistics.

To speak with an export counselor, contact the Bureau of Industry and Security at any of the following:
https://www.bis.doc.gov/index.php/about-bis/contact-bis

(202) 482-4811 - Outreach and Educational Services Division (located in Washington, DC)
(949) 660–0144 - Western Regional Office (located in Newport Beach, CA)
(408) 998-8806 - Northern California branch (located in San Jose, CA)

or e-mail your inquiry to the Export Counseling Division of the Office of Exporter Services at: ECDOEXS@bis.doc.gov

Bureau of Industry and Security home website:
www.bis.doc.gov

Want to know more about what U.S. Customs and Border Protection do? Read more on their website or contact them with a specific question:
http://www.cbp.gov/contact

ITAR (U.S. Department of State, Directorate of Defense Trade Controls) for specific questions:
https://www.pmddtc.state.gov/response_team/index.html

AES License Code Table:

http://kb.iesltd.com/index.php?article=157

Electronic Code of Federal Regulations (e-CFR)
http://www.ecfr.gov/cgi-bin/ECFR?page=browse

Title 15 Part 740 Exceptions (LVS, GBS, CIV, APP, TMP, RPL, GFT, BAG)

Alphabetical Index to the CCL (Commerce Control List)
http://www.avantinternational.com/sEARchableccl/2011-02-10_The_SEARchable_CCL.pdf

Country Chart
http://www.bis.doc.gov/index.php/forms-documents/doc_view/14-commerce-country-chart

EEI Codes
https://www.pld-certify.ups.com/CerttoolHelp/PLD0200/WebHelp_pld0200/EEI_Related_Codes_Values.htm

Harmonized Tariff Schedule
https://usitc.gov/tata/hts/bychapter/index.htm

Schedule B
http://www.census.gov/foreign-trade/schedules/b/index.html

*NOTE: Suggestions for online compliance solutions include but are not limited to Visual Compliance, Bis.doc.gov and more.

Other works by this author:

"Game Changer - MMORPG IRL: How to gain the gamer's edge"

"Better Luck Next Time: Nothing But Time Series" (Book 1); published 2016

Aralyn's blog site will have the updates on upcoming books and links to where they can be purchased at https://aralynblog.wordpress.com/

Follow her adventures in writing on her blog site, Facebook, Twitter, and G+

She's always happy when someone leaves a suggestion on what to write next or gives good critique.

Made in the USA
Columbia, SC
08 May 2019